1st Printing
September 2013

Karin Hauschild

Karin Hauschild has many years of
experience teaching a second language,
including English, German
and French, to university students
as well as to business executives.

She has written several books to help
students synthesize English learning,
in both grammar and sentence structure.

She has taught at private
language schools in the US and abroad,
and has tutored individual students
in IELTS, TOEFL & TOEIC preparation.
She currently teaches at
Northern Kentucky University.

English Sentence Patterns

is designed specifically for

international learners of

the English language to

help develop writing skills

for academic work

English
Sentence
Patterns

For additional information
and help with English writing,
visit our website
beaumondelang1.com

Contents

Transitions

Expressing Chronological Order
> first, second, then, meanwhile, finally, in the first place, next, after that, in the meantime, subsequently

Illustrating Previous Information
> in fact, indeed, actually as a matter of fact

Contradicting Previous Information
> but, on the other hand, nevertheless, yet, still, otherwise, however, in contrast, instead

Reducing the Importance of Previous Information
> anyway, at any rate, anyhow in any case

Indicating the Consequences of an Action
> so, therefore, as a result, consequently, thus

Expressing Reasons for an Action
> because, since

Expressing Concession or Condition
> although, even though, in spite of the fact that, even if

Making an Argument More Convincing
> and, as well as, plus, also, furthermore, to top it all off, in addition, besides, moreover, on top of that

Correcting Previous Information
> as a matter of fact, actually, in fact

Explaining Previous Information
> in other words, I mean, that is, for instance, for example, specifically

Verifying Previous Information
> really, naturally, certainly, indeed, of course

Summarizing
> so, in short, in conclusion, in the end, in summary, ultimately

Unit One

Sentence Components

Sentences consist of subjects, verbs, objects, complements, modifiers and connectors

Sentence Components

| Subject | Noun | *Flowers* bloom. |
| | Pronoun | *They* bloom. |

Verb		
	Simple present	Flowers *bloom.*
	Present continuous	Flowers *are blooming.*
	Simple past	Flowers *bloomed.*
	Past continuous	Flowers *were blooming.*
	Simple future	Flowers *will bloom.*
		Flowers *are going to* bloom.
	Future continuous	Flowers *will be blooming.*
		Flowers *are going to be blooming.*
	Present perfect	Flowers *have bloomed.*
	Present perfect continuous	Flowers *have been blooming.*
	Past perfect	Flowers *had bloomed.*
	Past perfect continuous	Flowers *had been blooming.*
	Future perfect	Flowers *will have bloomed.*
	Future perfect continuous	Flowers *will have been blooming.*

| Object | Noun | The woman picked *flowers.* |
| | Pronoun | The woman picked *them.* |

Complement	Noun	He is an *architect.*
	Pronoun	The man knows *it.*
	Adjective	She is *intelligent.*

Modifier	Adjective	*Yellow* flowers bloom.
	Adverb	Flowers bloom *freely.*
	Phrase	They bloom *in the garden.*
	Clause	*Despite the weather*, flowers bloom.

Connector	Coordinating conjunction	Flowers bloom *and* grow.
	Subordinating conjunction	Flowers bloom *because of* the sun.
	Correlative conjunction	Flowers *not only grow but also bloom.*

Unit Two

The Simple Sentence

A simple sentence has a noun subject
or a pronoun subject
and a verb in one of twelve tenses

Pattern 1

The Basic Simple Sentence

The basic simple sentence
has one subject and
one verb.

Flowers   bloom.
subject   *verb*

Pattern 2

The Simple Sentence with one Subject Modifier

The simple sentence with
one subject modifier has
an *adjective* that describes the
subject.

Spring flowers
adjective **subject**

bloom.
verb

Pattern 3

The Simple Sentence with Two or More Subject Modifiers

The simple sentence with
two or more subject
modifiers has two or more
adjectives that describe the
subject.

Beautiful spring
adjective   *adjective*
flowers bloom.
subject   *verb*

Pattern 1	Write basic simple sentences
Pattern 2	Write simple sentences with one subject modifier
Pattern 3	Write simple sentences with two or more subject modifiers

Pattern 4

The Simple Sentence with One Verb Modifier

The simple sentence with one verb modifier has an *adverb* that describes the verb.

Flowers   bloom
subject   *verb*

gently.
adverb

Pattern 5

The Simple Sentence with Two or More Verb Modifiers

The simple sentence with two or more verb modifiers has two or more *adverbs* that describe the verb.

Flowers bloom
subject   *verb*

gently
adverb

and

elegantly.
adverb

Pattern 6

The Simple Sentence with Multiple Subject & Verb Modifiers

The simple sentence with multiple subject & verb modifiers has *adjectives* that describe the subject and *adverbs* that describe the verb.

Beautiful spring
adjective   *adjective*

flowers bloom gently
subject   *verb*   *adverb*

and elegantly.
adverb

Pattern 4   *Write simple sentences with one verb modifier*

Pattern 5   *Write simple sentences with two or more verb modifiers*

Pattern 6   *Write sentences with multiple subject and verb modifiers*

Pattern 7

The Simple Sentence with Prepositional Phrase Modifiers

The simple sentence with prepositional phrase modifiers has prepositional phrases that describe the *subject* and/or the *verb*

Flowers on the vine
subject   prepositional phrase

are blooming
verb

in the garden.
prepositional phrase

Pattern 8

The Simple Sentence with Present Participial Phrase Modifiers

The simple sentence with present participial phrase modifiers has present participial phrases that describe the *subject* and/or the *verb*

Flowers,
subject

blooming this spring,
present participial phrase

have grown,
verb

providing shade.
present participial phrase

Pattern 7   *Write simple sentences with preposi-*
                 tional phrase modifiers

Pattern 8   *Write simple sentences with present*
                 participial phrase modifiers

Pattern 9

The Simple Sentence with Past Participial Phrase Modifiers

The simple sentence with past participial phrase modifiers has past participial phrases that describe the subject and/or the verb

Flowers,
subject

planted this spring,
past participial phrase

are blooming.
verb

Pattern 10

The Simple Sentence with Infinitive Phrase Modifiers

The simple sentence with infinitive phrase modifiers has infinitive phrases that describe the verb

Flowers
subject

are blooming
verb

to give pleasure.
infinitive phrase

10

Pattern 9   *Write simple sentences with past participial phrase modifiers*

Pattern 10   *Write simple sentences with infinitive phrase modifiers*

The Simple Sentence with a Combination of Modifiers

The simple sentence with a combination of modifiers has has *adjectives, adverbs,* prepositional phrases, present participial phrases, *past participial phrases,* and *infinitive phrases,* that describe the subject and the verb

Beautiful spring
adjective   adjective

flowers,
subject

planted last fall,
past participial phrase

are blooming
verb

gently and
adverb

elegantly
adverb

in the garden,
prepositional phrase

bending in the breeze,
present participial phrase

to create color.
infinitive phrase

Simple Sentence Samples

My house was on the side of a hill, on the edge of the large wood, in the middle of a young forest of pines, near the pond, to which a narrow path led down the hill.

Here comes the cattle train bearing the cattle of a thousand hills, whirled along like leaves blown from the mountains by the September gales.

I looked between and over the near green hills to some distant and higher ones on the horizon, tinged with blue.

Pattern 11   *Write simple sentences with a combination of modifiers*

Simple Sentence Patterns

Write simple sentences using different modifiers that describe the subjects and the verbs

The Compound Sentence

A compound sentence has two or more
subject & verb combinations joined
by a coordinating conjunction:
and, or, but, so, for, yet, nor

Pattern 1

The Basic Compound Sentence

The basic compound sentence has two subjects and two verbs joined by a coordinating conjunction.

Flowers bloom
subject　　*verb*

and
coordinating conjunction

rain drizzles.
subject　　*verb*

Pattern 2

The Compound Sentence with Subject Modifiers

The compound sentence with subject modifiers has two or more adjectives that describe the subjects.

Beautiful flowers bloom
adjective　　*subject*　　*verb*

but
coordinating conjunction

the cold wind blows.
adjective　*subject*　　*verb*

Pattern 3

The Compound Sentence with Verb Modifiers

The compound sentence with verb modifiers has two or more adverbs that describe the verbs.

Flowers bloomed gently
subject　　*verb*　　*adverb*

but
coordinating conjunction

the wind
subject

blew fiercely.
verb　　*adverb*

16

Pattern 1	*Write basic compound sentences*

Pattern 2	*Write compound sentences with subject modifiers*

Pattern 3	*Write compound sentences with verb modifiers*

17

Pattern 4

The Compound Sentence with Subject & Verb Modifiers

The compound sentence with subject & verb modifiers has adjectives and adverbs that describe the subjects and the verbs.

Beautiful red **flowers**
adjective   *adjective*   **subject**

bloom copiously
verb   *adverb*

yet
coordinating conjunction

the bitter cold **wind**
adjective   *adjective*   **subject**

blows relentlessly.
verb   *adverb*

Pattern 5

The Compound Sentence with Prepositional Phrase Subject Modifiers

The compound sentence with prepositional phrase subject modifiers has prepositional phrases that describe the subjects.

The flowers
subject

in the garden
prepositional phrase

bloom gently,
verb   *adverb*

for
coordinating conjunction

the wind
subject

from the south
prepositional phrase

blows softly.
verb   *adverb*

Pattern 4   *Write compound sentences with subject and verb modifiers*

Pattern 5   *Write compound sentences with prepositional phrase subject modifiers*

Pattern 6

The Compound Sentence with Prepositional Phrase Verb Modifiers

The compound sentence with prepositional phrase verb modifiers has prepositional phrases that describe the verbs.

Flowers bloom
subject   verb

by the gate,
prepositional phrase

but
coordinating conjunction

the wind blows
subject   verb

from the north.
prepositional phrase

Pattern 7

The Compound Sentence with Present Participial Phrase Subject Modifiers

The compound sentence with present participial phrase subject modifiers has present participial phrases that describe the subjects.

Flowers
subject

growing this spring
present participial phrase

are colorful,
verb   adjective

yet
coordinating conjunction

the wind
subject

blowing fiercely
present participial phrase

is cold.
verb   adjective

Pattern 6 *Write compound sentences with prepositional phrase verb modifiers*

Pattern 7 *Write compound sentences with present participial phrase subject modifiers*

Pattern 8

The Compound Sentence with Past Participial Phrase Subject Modifiers

The compound sentence with past participial phrase subject modifiers has *past participial phrases* that describe the subjects.

The flowers
subject

planted this spring
past participial phrase

have bloomed quickly,
verb   *adverb*

but
coordinating conjunction

the plants
subject

bought this fall
past participial phrase

are growing slowly.
verb   *adverb*

Pattern 9

The Compound Sentence with Infinitive Phrase Verb Modifiers

The compound sentence with infinitive phrase verb modifiers has *infinitive phrases* that describe the verbs.

Flowers bloom
subject   *verb*

to make the world nicer,
infinitive phrase

but
coordinating conjunction

the wind blows
subject   *verb*

to cool the air.
infinitive phrase

Pattern 8   *Write compound sentences with past participial subject modifiers*

Pattern 9   *Write compound sentences with infinitive phrase verb modifiers*

23

Pattern 10

The Compound Sentence with a Combination of Modifiers

The compound sentence with a combination of modifiers uses a combination of *adjectives*, *adverbs*, prepositional phrases, present & past participial phrases, and *infinitive phrases* to describe the subjects and the verbs.

Bright red summer
adjective   adjective   adjective

flowers
subject

bloom gracefully
verb   adverb

by the front gate,
prepositional phrase

and
coordinating conjunction

a gentle breeze,
adjective   subject

coming from the south,
present participial phrase

blows lightly
verb   adverb

over the roses
prepositional phrase

attached to the old fence
past participial phrase

to support
infinitive phrase

the climbing blossoms.

The rain was now over, and a rainbow above the eastern woods promised a fair evening, so I set out on my journey gladly and with anticipation.

24

Pattern 10   *Write compound sentences with a combination of modifiers*

Compound Sentence Patterns

Write compound sentences using different modifiers that describe the subjects and the verbs

Unit Four

The Complex Sentence

A complex sentence has one independent subject/verb clause and one or more dependent clauses introduced by subordinate conjunctions such as: *when, because, after, before, while, as, since, as soon as, until, now that, by the time, once, as long as, whenever, every time, even though, even if, whether or not, in case, unless, only if, whereas, although*

Pattern 1

The Basic Complex Sentence

The basic complex sentence has one independent clause and one dependent clause.

Flowers bloom
independent clause
while the wind blows.
dependent clause

Pattern 2

The Complex Sentence with Subject Modifiers

The complex sentence with subject modifiers has *adjectives* that describe the subjects of the independent clause and the dependent clause.

Gorgeous yellow flowers bloom
independent clause
while the soft wind blows.
dependent clause

Pattern 3

The Complex Sentence with Verb Modifiers

The complex sentence with verb modifiers has *adverbs* that describe the verb in the independent clause and the dependent clause.

Flowers bloom freely
independent clause
as the wind blows gently.
dependent clause

Pattern 1	*Write basic complex sentences*

Pattern 2	*Write complex sentences with subject modifiers*

Pattern 3	**Write complex sentences with verb modifiers**

Pattern 4

The Complex Sentence with Subject & Verb Modifiers

The complex sentence with subject and verb modifiers has *adjectives* that describe the subjects and *adverbs* that describe the verbs in the independent and the dependent clauses

Gorgeous yellow **flowers bloom** freely
independent clause

because the soft **rain falls** gently.
dependent clause

Pattern 5

The Complex Sentence with Prepositional Phrase Subject Modifiers

The complex sentence with prepositional phrase subject modifiers has *prepositional phrases* that describe the subjects in the independent clause and the dependent clause

Flowers in the garden bloom
independent clause

as long as the season of summer lasts.
dependent clause

Pattern 6

The Complex Sentence with Prepositional Phrase Verb Modifiers

The complex sentence with prepositional phrase verb modifiers has *prepositional phrases* that describe the verbs in the independent clause and the dependent clause

Flowers grew near the gate,
independent clause

even though the wind blew from the south.
dependent clause

Pattern 4 *Write complex sentences with subject and verb modifiers*

Pattern 5 *Write complex sentences with prepositional phrase subject modifiers*

Pattern 6 *Write complex sentences with prepositional phrase verb modifiers*

Pattern 7

The Complex Sentence with Present Participial Phrase Subject & Verb Modifiers

The complex sentence with present participial phrase subject and verb modifiers has present participial phrases that describe the subjects and the verbs in the independent clause and /or the dependent clause

Flowers, growing freely, close

independent clause

every time night falls, cooling the air.

dependent clause

Pattern 8

The Complex Sentence with Past Participial Phrase Subject & Verb Modifiers

The complex sentence with past participial phrase subject and verb modifiers has past participial phrases that describe the subjects and verbs in the independent clause and/or the dependent clause

Flowers, planted last year, bloom

independent clause

before the winter comes, filled with snow.

dependent clause

Pattern 7   *Write complex sentences with present participial prase subject and verb modifiers*

Pattern 8   *Write comploex sentences with past participial phrase subject and verb modifiers*

Pattern 9

The Complex Sentence with Infinitive Phrase Verb Modifiers

The complex sentence with infinitive phrase modifiers has *infinitive phrases* **that describe** the purpose of the verbs in the independent clause and /or the dependent clause

Flowers are planted
to please us,
independent clause
whereas the wind blows
to destroy the garden.
dependent clause

Pattern 10

The Complex Sentence with a Combination of Modifiers

The complex sentence with a combination of modifiers uses *adjectives*, *adverbs*, **prepo-**sitional phrases, present and *past participial phrases* and *infinitive phrases* **to describe** the subjects and verbs in the independent clause and/or the dependent clause

Colorful purple **flowers,**

growing

near the fence,

blow freely

in the wind,

while a gentle **breeze,**

cooled **by the** night **air,**

playfully **brushes the**
vines

as it gently **passes**

through the garden

to caress the plants.

34

Pattern 9

Write complex sentences with infinitive phrase verb modifiers

Pattern 10 *Write complex sentences with a combination of modifiers*

Unit Five

The Compound-Complex Sentence

A compound-complex sentence has two or more independent clauses and one or more dependent clauses

These sentences can use both coordinating and/or subordinating conjunctions

Pattern 1

The Basic Compound-Complex Sentence

The basic compound-complex sentence has two or more independent clauses and one or more dependent clauses

Flowers bloom
independent clause
though the storm destroys
dependent clause
and the wind blows
independent clause
while the sun shines.
dependent clause

Pattern 2

The Compound-Complex Sentence with Subject Modifiers

The compound-complex sentence with subject modifiers has one or more *adjectives* that describe the subjects in the independent and the dependent clauses

Spring flowers bloom
adjective
though a strong storm threatens
adjective
and the wild wind blows
adjective
while the pale sun shines.
adjective

Pattern 3

The Compound-Complex Sentence with Verb Modifiers

The compound-complex sentence with verb modifiers has one or more *adverbs* that describe the verbs in the independent and the dependent clauses

Flowers bloom brightly
adverb
now that spring has

finally arrived,
adverb
but yet the wind blows fiercely
adverb
while the sun barely appears.
adverb

38

Pattern 1   *Write basic compound-complex*
sentences

Pattern 2   *Write compound-complex sentences*
with subject modifiers

Pattern 3   *Write compound-complex sentences*
with verb modifiers

Pattern 4

The Compound-Complex Sentence with Subject & Verb Modifiers

The compound-complex sentence with subject & verb modifiers has *adjectives* that describe the nouns and *adverbs* that describe the verbs in the independent and dependent clauses

Spring flowers
adjective
bloom abundantly
adverb
although the cold wind
adjective
blows relentlessly,
adverb
and the pale sun
adjective
warms ceaselessly,
adverb
as the new day calmly dawns
adjective   *adverb*

Pattern 5

The Compound-Complex Sentence with Prepositional Phrase Subject Modifiers

The compound-complex sentence with prepositional phrase subject modifiers has prepositional phrases that describe the subjects in the independent and the dependent clauses

The flowers

in the garden
prepositional phrase
are blooming,

even though

the wind from the north
prepositional phrase
is blowing

as clouds

gather ominously

Pattern 4   *Write compound-complex sentences with subject and verb modifiers*

Pattern 5   *Write compound-complex sentences with prepositional phrase subject modifiers*

Pattern 6

The Compound-Complex Sentence with Prepositional Phrase Verb Modifiers

The compound-complex sentence with prepositional phrase verb modifiers have prepositional phrases that describe the verbs in the independent and dependent clauses

Roses

bloom in the garden,
prepositional phrase
but the wind

blows cold from the west,
prepositional phrase
as day

fades into night
prepositional phrase

Pattern 7

The Compound-Complex Sentence with Present Participial Phrase Subject Modifiers

The compound-complex sentence with present participial subject modifiers has present participial phrases that describe the subjects in the independent and the dependent clauses

Flowers,

blooming along the fence,
present participial phrase
grow slowly,

because the wind,

blowing ceaselessly
present participial phrase
prevents their blossoming,

nor is the weather,

changing daily,
present participial phrase
warm enough

Pattern 6 *Write compound-complex sentences
with prepositional phrase verb modifiers*

Pattern 7 *Write compound-complex sentences
with present participial phrase subject
modifiers*

Pattern 8

The Compound-Complex Sentence with Present Participial Phrase Verb Modifiers

The compound-complex sentence with present participial phrase verb modifiers has present participial phrases that describe the verbs in the independent and dependent clauses

Flowers bloom profusely,

providing many colors,
present participial phrase
even though

the wind blows steadily,

freezing the petals,
present participial phrase
and the night descends slowly,

darkening the valley
present participial phrase

Pattern 9

The Compound-Complex Sentence with Past Participial Phrase Subject Modifiers

The compound-complex sentence with past participial subject modifiers has *past participial phrases* that describe the subjects in the independent and the dependent clauses

Flowers,

planted this spring,
past participial phrase
will bloom in the fall,

while the trees,

stripped of their leaves,
past participial phrase
bend low in the wind

44

Pattern 8   *Write compound-complex sentences with present participial phrase verb modifiers*

Pattern 9   *Write compound-complex sentences with past participial phrase subject modifiers*

Pattern 10

The Compound-Complex Sentence with Infinitive Phrase Verb Modifiers

The compound-complex sentence with infinitive phrase verb modifiers has *infinitive phrases* that describe the verbs in the independent and dependent clauses

The flowers

are blooming early

to provide color,
infinitive phrase
yet the wind

blows relentlessly,

to prevent their growth
infinitive phrase
during a season of change

Pattern 11

The Compound-Complex Sentence with a Combination of Modifiers

The compound-complex sentence with a combination of modifiers has adjectives, *adverbs*, prepositional phrases, present and *past* participial phrases, and *infinitive phrases* that describe the subjects and/or the verbs in the independent and the dependent clauses

The flowers in the garden

bloom gracefully
adverb
despite the bad weather
adjective
bringing rain
present participial phrase
to a southern garden,
prepositional phrase
carefully tended,
past participial phrase
even as the wind blows

to caress the garden,
infinitive phrase
until the day dawns

46

Pattern 10   *Write compound-complex sentences with infinitive phrase verb modifiers*

Pattern 11   *Write compound-complex sentences with a combination of modifiers*

The following units develop the writing

of the four basic sentences

into more complex forms

to provide the writer

with additional techniques to use

in creating writing of academic quality

Unit Six

The Combined Sentence

*Short sentences can be combined
into one longer sentence,
keeping all the important parts,
including adjectives, adverbs, phrases and clauses
The finished sentence should reflect
the intent and feeling of the original sentences*

49

Adding Adjectives & Adverbs
to the Basic Sentence Unit

> A man gave me a drawing.
> It was of a young woman.
> The man was old.
> It was faded.
> The woman's eyes were sad.
> The drawing brought back memories.
> They were from a long time ago.
> The memories made me happy.

An old man gave me a faded drawing of a young woman with sad eyes, bringing back memories from a long time ago, making me happy.

Sentence Sample 2

Adding Prepositional Phrases
to the Basic Sentence Unit

> A man stood, looking down.
> He stood on a railroad bridge.
> He was looking down into the water.
> The water was twenty feet below.
> The water was swift.
> The water was turbulent.

A man stood on a railroad bridge looking down into the swift turbulent water twenty feet below.

Adding Coordinating Words, Phrases & Clauses
to the Basic Sentence Unit

> The wind became gentle.
> The rain became a mist.
> The clouds cleared.
> The sun shone through.
> It was a beautiful day.
> I was outside.
> I was in our garden.

I was outside in our garden when the winds became gentle, the rain became a mist, and the clouds cleared, letting the sun shine through, making it a beautiful day.

Adding Adverb Clauses
to the Basic Sentence Unit

> Some day I shall wander.
> I shall go out into the meadow.
> The meadow is beautiful.
> I shall do this when the clouds are dark.
> I shall do this when the rain is falling.
> I shall do this when the wind is blowing.

Some day, when the clouds are dark, the rain is falling, and the wind is blowing, I shall go out into the beautiful meadow to wander.

Sentence Practice 1

Combine the following sentences into a single sentence

I lived alone.
I lived in the woods.
I lived a mile from any neighbor.
I lived in a house I build myself.
I lived there for two years.

Sentence Practice 2

Human nature has fine qualities.
It is similar to ripe fruit.
It must be handled delicately.
We do not treat ourselves tenderly.
We do not treat one another kindly.

Sentence Practice 3

Most people live in desperation.
This desperation is quiet.
It is resignation.
It is an unconscious despair.
It is hidden by the pursuit
of idle entertainment.

Sample answers can be found on pages 56 - 57

Sentence Practice 1

Sentence Practice 2

Sentence Practice 3

Sentence Practice 4

Combine the following sentences into a single sentence

We must consider what the chief
purpose of mankind is.
It is not too late.
We have to give up prejudices.
We have to have proof.
None of our thinking can be trusted.
What is true today, may not be
true tomorrow.

Sentence Practice 5

I have been anxious to value time.
I have appreciated it in any weather.
I have appreciated it at any time.
I have stood on the edge of eternity.
The past and the future have met.
That is the present moment.

Sentence Practice 6

We want to succeed.
We are in a hurry to become
successful.
We do not need to keep up
with anyone.
We need to consider our own
thoughts.
We need to follow our own paths.

Sample answers can be found on pages 56 - 57

Sentence Practice 4

Sentence Practice 5

Sentence Practice 6

1

I lived in the woods alone for two years, a mile from any neighbor, in a house I built myself.

For two years, I lived in the woods alone, in a house I built myself, a mile from any neighbor.

For two years, I lived alone in the woods, a mile from any neighbor, in a house I built myself.

2

The quality of human nature is similar to ripe fruit, and must be handled delicately, as we treat ourselves tenderly, and one another kindly.

Human nature has the quality of ripe fruit, needing to be handled delicately, as we treat ourselves and one another tenderly and kindly.

Human nature has a fine quality similar to ripe fruit and needs to be handled delicately in our treatment of ourselves and others with kindness and tenderness.

3

Most people live in quiet desperation, in a kind of resignation, an unconscious despair, which they try to hide by pur suing idle entertainment.

Most people experience a kind of resignation, a quiet desperation and an unconscious despair, which they ignore by engaging in constant entertainment.

4

It is not too late to consider what the chief purpose of mankind is, as we give up our prejudices, not trusting our own thinking, which may be true today but which may not be true tomorrow.

It is not too late to consider what the chief purpose of mankind is, relinguishing our prejudices, and not trusting our thinking, because it may not be true tomorrow even if it is true today.

5

I have been anxious to value time in any weather, and at any time, having stood on the edge of eternity, where the past and future meet in the present moment.

To value time at any given moment, in any kind of weather, is to stand on the edge of eternity, allowing the present moment to intertwine the past with the future.

6

In our desire to become successful, we attempt to keep up with others, but we need only to consider our own thoughts, and to follow our own paths.

We need not keep up with others to succeed, but only to follow our own thoughts and paths.

Evaluating Sentence Combining

Meaning

It is important to express the idea intended by the original author

Coherence

The parts of the sentence must fit together logically and smoothly

Conciseness

The sentence must express an idea without wasting words

Clarity

The sentence must be understood when first read

Emphasis

The key words and phrases must be in order of importance

Rhythm

The sentence must have flow and must move smoothly.

Unit Seven

The Expanded Sentence

The subjects, objects and verbs of sentences
can be expande with
descriptive phrases

Expanded Subjects

A sentence with an expanded subject has a descriptive phrase modifying the subject noun

The boy over there, *the one in the green shirt*, is my sister's friend.

The ball the children played with, *the only one available*, was large and bright red.

Expanded Verbs

A sentence with an expanded verb has a descriptive phrase modifying the verb

The class read the story, *without interest at first, then with increasing attention.*

We ran out of the rain *with speed and agitation*, making sure we were safely inside before the storm.

Expanded Objects

A sentence with an expanded object has a descriptive phrase modifying the object

We watched the tennis star, *athletic and strong*, winning his tenth championship match.

The child, *unusually quiet, relaxed and intent*, watched the exciting movie before going willingly to bed.

Write sentences with expanded subjects

Expanded Verbs Practice

Write sentences with expanded Verbs

Expanded Objects Practice

Write sentences with expanded objects

Sample Sentences with Expanded Subjects, Verbs & Objects

One starry night, *a million years ago, it seems,* she watched the waves roll in along the African shore.

He walked along the shore, *lost in thought, not noticing the incoming* tide.

The child, *alone and lost,* hugged the little dog, *whimpering softly.*

The stars, *twinkling merrily,* guided his journey through the dense forest, *filled with mystery.*

After he had read the book, *full of wonder and delight,* he began to dream and make his plans, *without fear.*

Once upon a time, *a time lost to memory and beyond recall,* he had visited a beautiful country, *long familiar in his imagination,* and now entirely visible, *revealed in all its splendor.*

Deep in the forest, *lonely and quiet,* where shadows shimmer, *unseen and hidden,* where dappled light glimmers and dances, where the wildwood whispers its secrets, lived a child name Clara, *loved by everyone.*

The starlit sky looked down, *watchfully and caringly,* on the child, *sleeping softly in the grass,* whose dreams, *filled with magic experienced each day,* gave him peaceful sleep and joy.

Unit Eight

The Periodic Sentence

The periodic sentence has three forms:
* *<u>The basic periodic</u>, which includes additional details before the basic sentence is complete*
* *<u>The interrupted periodic</u>, in which additional details are added within the basic statement*
* *<u>The loose periodic</u>, in which a string of details is added to a basic statement*

The Basic Periodic Sentence

In the basic periodic sentence, modifying details are placed before the completion of the statement

<u>Basic Sentence:</u> John gave his mother flowers.

<u>Basic Periodic Sentence:</u> John, *usually the tough one, the normally sullen boy, who refused to show any feelings,* gave his mother flowers.

The Interrupted Periodic Sentence

In the interrupted periodic sentence, modifying details are added within the basic statement

<u>Basic Sentence:</u> Love is blind.

<u>Interrupted Periodic Sentence:</u> Love, *as everyone knows, except those who happen to be in love,* is blind.

The Loose Periodic Sentence

In the loose periodic sentence, modifying details are added in a series, following the basic sentence

<u>Basic Sentence:</u> Bells rang.

<u>Loose Periodic Sentence:</u> Bells rang, *filling the air with their noisy clanging, startling birds from their roosts, bringing people into the streets to hear the news.*

Basic Periodic Sentence Practice

Write basic periodic sentences

Interrupted Periodic Sentence Practice

Write interrupted periodic sentences

Loose Periodic Sentence Practice

Write loose periodic sentences

Sample Basic, Interrupted & Loose
Periodic Sentences

The little boy, *the one who never cried, was never afraid nor aggressive*, was always kind to his teammates.

The woman's husband, *never late with a gift for her birthday*, forgot to give her a present this year.

The summer sky, *continually bright, forever starry*, lit their way through the forest.

The news, *reported by the local papers making sure of delivery*, was sensational that day.

The children, *creating teams, challenging each other, allowing everyone to play*, interacted cooperatively.

The test, *creating anguish for the students, causing many to fail*, was difficult.

The summer flowers bloomed, *creating a colorful canopy, enriching the garden, giving pleasure to everyone*.

Love is anguish, *ensnaring everyone in its tentacles, causing pain every day, depressing the spirit, and leading to depression*.

The music flowed, *encompassing the spirit of the listeners, allowing them to imagine a better world, wrapping them in ecstacy*.

Unit Nine

The Cumulative Sentence

The cumulative sentence adds details both before and after the basic statement

The Cumulative Sentence

*In the cumulative sentence, modifying details
are added before and after the basic statement*

John was angry.
basic sentence

John was suddenly, violently angry.
periodic sentence/detail added before ending adjective

John, usually a very calm man,
was suddenly, violently angry.
periodic sentence/appositive describing subject

John, usually a very calm man,
was suddenly, violently angry,
so angry that he lost complete control.
ending detail/adding information

Usually a very calm man,
John was suddenly, violently angry,
so angry that he lost complete control
of his feelings.
beginning detail/describing subject

Cumulative Sentence Practice

Write cumulative sentences

The roof tile fell.

The roof tile suddenly fell.

After one hundred years, the roof tile suddenly and without warning fell in the night.

After one hundred years, buffeted by wind and rain, the roof tile suddenly and without warning fell in the night.

After one hundred years, constantly buffeted by fierce wind and rain, the loose roof tile fell suddenly and without warning onto the steet in the night.

After one hundred long years, constantly buffeted by fierce wind and icy rain, the ancient roof tile, which had been loose for decades, fell suddenly and without warning onto the street in the night and into the path of a young girl.

After one hundred long, lonely years, constantly buffeted by fierce wind and icy rain, the ancient and historic roof tile, which had been loose for decades, fell suddenly and without warning onto the quiet and deserted street in the still night and into the path of an unsuspecting young girl.

After one hundred long, lonely, forgotten years, constantly buffeted by fierce wind and icy rain, the ancient and historic roof tile, which had been loose for decades, fell suddenly, silently and without warning onto the quiet and deserted street in the still night, and into the path of an unsuspecting young girl, who picked it up and took it home.

After one hundred long, lonely, forgotten years, constantly buffeted by fierce wind and icy rain, the ancient and historic roof tile, which had been loose for decades and threatening to fall, fell suddenly, silently and without warning, onto the quiet and deserted street in the still and motionless night, and into the path of an unsuspecting young girl, who picked it up and took it home to give t o her mother as a gift, who treasured it and placed it on the old mantel.

The Parallel Sentence

Parallel structure is used to produce a balanced sentence, creating clarity and equality in the importance of ideas, and rhythm in expression

Parallelism with Nouns

Incorrect:	The wind blew, the rain fell, and it was bad weather.
Correct:	The wind blew, the rain fell, and the weather was bad.

Parallelism with Adjectives

Incorrect:	The vacation was pleasant, entertaining, and we did a lot of things.
Correct:	The vacation was pleasant, entertaining and full of activity.

Parallelism with Adverbs

Incorrect:	They worked hard, carefully and with energy.
Correct:	They worked hard, carefully and energetically.

Parallelism with Verb Tenses

Incorrect:	We walked through the woods, picked wild blueberries, and are now home.
Correct:	We walked through the woods, picked wild blueberries and went home.

Parallel Sentence Practice

Write a parallel sentence using a noun

Write a parallel sentence using an adjective

Write a parallel sentence using an adverb

Write a parallel sentence using a verb tense

Parallelism with Gerunds

Incorrect: Reading, listening to music and to watch TV are relaxing.

Correct: Reading, listening to music and watching TV are relaxing.

Parallelism with Infinitives

Incorrect: I want to travel, visit historical sites, and and learn about different cultures.

Correct: I want to travel, to visit historical sites, and to learn about different cultures.

Parallelism with Comparisons

Incorrect: He would rather sail the ocean than going whitewater rafting.

Correct: He would rather sail the ocean than go whitewater rafting.

Parallelism with Prepositional Phrases

Incorrect: The sun shone on the garden, the trees and in the water.

Correct: The sun shone on the water, on the trees and on the water.

Parallel Sentence Practice

Write a parallel sentence using a gerund

Write a parallel sentence using an infinitive

Write a parallel sentence using a comparison

Write a parallel sentence using a prepositional phrase

Parallelism with Independent Clauses

Incorrect: The people voted to build a new library, but don't know how to finance it.

Correct: The people voted to build a new library, but they didn't know how to finance it.

Parallelism with Subordinate Clauses

Incorrect: She graduated from school with honors, when she had gone to live in Europe.

Correct: She graduated from school with honors, before she went to live in Europe.

Parallelism with Coordinating Conjunctions

Incorrect: The winter arrived arrived suddenly and with bitter cold.

Correct: The winter arrived suddenly and brought bitter cold with it.

Parallelism with Correlative Conjunctions

Incorrect: He not only studied ancient languages, but also ancient history.

Correct: He studied not only ancient languages, but also ancient history.

Parallel Sentence Practice

Write a parallel sentence using an independent clause

Write a parallel sentence using a subordinate clause

Write a parallel sentence using a coordinating conjunction

Write a parallel sentence using a correlative conjunction

Parallelism with a Series

Incorrect:	It was a great day, a wonderful night, and we enjoyed it.
Correct:	It was a great day, a wonderful night, and an enjoyable time.

Parallelism with Linking Verbs

Incorrect:	He appeared to be a success, and was proud.
Correct:	He appeared to be a success, and to be a proud man.

Sample Parallel Structure Sentences

I have occasional visits in the long winter evenings, when the snow falls fast and the wind howls in the woods.

Sometimes I rambled further westward, or, while the sun was setting, made a supper of blueberries on the hill.

The rain was now over, and a rainbow above the eastern wood promised a fair evening, so I set out on my journey gladly and with anticipation.

The life in us is like the water in the river, rising higher this year than man has ever known, and flooding the parched uplands.

Parallel Sentence Practice

Write a parallel sentence using a series

Write a parallel sentence using a linking verb

Write parallel sentences using a variety of techniques

Sample Parallel Structure Sentences

At length the winter came in good earnest, and the wind began to howl around the house, as if it had not had permission to do so before.

On warm evenings, I frequently sat in my boat playing the flute, and saw the moon traveling over the water.

The pond was completely surrounded by thick and lofty pines and oaks, and in some of its coves grape vines had run over the trees next to the water and formed bowers under which a boat could pass.

My house was on the side of a hill, on the edge of the large wood, in the middle of a young forest of pines, near the pond, to which a narrow path led down the hill.

This small lake was of most value during a gentle rainstorm in August, both air and water being perfectly still, the sky overcast and the evening serene.

A lake like this is never smoother than at such a time, made shallow and dark by clouds, with the water full of light and reflection.

The light which puts out our eyes is darkness to us and only that day dawns to which we are awake, since there is more day to dawn, the sun being but a morning star.

Unit Eleven

Variety in Sentences

*Different methods can be used
to create variety in sentences:
sentence beginnings
sentence length
repetition
transitions
gerund/infinitive joining
modifiers*

Variety in Sentence Beginnings

Adverb: Suddenly the rain began to pour
                                down.

Prepositional   In the evening, they played cards
Phrase: together.

Adjective: Beautiful and calm, the lake
                                shimmered in the sunlight.

Present Participial   Deciding to go for a walk, they
Phrase: set out early in the evening.

Past participial   Delapidated and broken, the gate
Phrase: swung loosely.

Adverb Clause: Despite the lateness of the hour,
                                they still continued reading.

Verb: Try hard to succeed.

Gerund: Loving our children is a great joy.

Infinitive: To begin a new day is a pleasure.

Correlative   Whether or not we go to town is
Conjunction: not important.

Subject: The dawn surprised us with its
                                brilliant colors.

Variety in Sentence Beginnings

Write sentences using a variety of beginnings

Variety in Sentence Length

She called out suddenly. In his surprise, he did not immediately realize that she needed his help.

I find it wholesome to be alone the greater part of the time. To be in company, even with the best, is soon wearisome and dissipating. I love to be alone. I never found the companion that was so companionable as solitude.

Variety in Repetition

The quiet end of the day, when the sunset colored the whole world, the sunset that we had awaited eagerly all day, the sunset that we had thought we would never see again, gave us a strange peace.

Variety in Transitions

Using different transitional vocabulary with similar meanings creates variety in sentences: *however, moreover, nevertheless, but, therefore.*
Placing various transitions in different positions in the sentences produces variety.

Variety through -ing/ed Joining

He thought the day would never end, feeling as though he had traveled a great distance and noticing that the end of the journey was approaching.
He thought the day would never end, troubled and disturbed in his impression that the road, long traveled, would continue forever.

Variety in Sentence Length

Write long and short sentences

Variety in Repetition

Write a sentence with repetition

Variety in Transitions

Write sentences using a variety of transitions

Variety through ing/ed Joining

Write a sentence using ing/ed joining

Variety through Modifiers

Appositives:
The man, the one who had given her the roses, met her at the gate.

Relative Clause:
The woman who had given me her umbrella joined us on our walk.

Beginning with a Modifier:
Violent but beautiful, the storm came suddenly, surprising us.

Ending with a Modifier:
The road appeared long and desolate before us, wandering continuously uphill.

Placing a Modifier in the Middle:
The forest, dark, dim and dense, presented a frightening appearance as we continued on our journey.

Modifier Chain:
The boy, small and helpless, not much older than ten, but wiry and athletic, jumped the stream easily.

Summative Modifiers:
It seemed as if she would stay there forever, watching the ocean waves roll in, sitting quietly on the beach, not knowing that someone was watching her from the path.

Variety through Modifiers

Write sentences using a variety of modifiers

I am convinced, both by faith and experience, that to maintain one's self on this earth is not a hardship but a pastime, if we will live simply and wisely.

This small lake was of most value as a neighbor in the intervals of a gentle rainstorm in August, when, both air and water being perfectly still, but the sky over-cast, mid-afternoon had all the serenity of evening, and the wood thrush sang around, and was heard from shore to shore.

Every morning was a cheerful invitation to make my life of equal simplicity, and I may say innocence, with nature herself.

Some of my pleasantest hours were during the long rainstorms in the spring or fall,which confined me to the house for the afternoon as well as the forenoon, soothed by their ceaseless roar and peltings; when an early twilight ushered in a long evening in which many thoughts had time to take root and unfold themselves.

Time is but the stream I go fishing in. I drink at it; but while I drink I see the sandy bottom and detect how shallow it is. Its thin current slides away, but eternity remains.

Sometimes on Sundays, I heard the bells, when the wind was favorable, a faint, sweet, and, as it were, natural melody, worth importing into the wilderness.

Unit Twelve

Literary Sentences

*Literary terms give sentences
an added dimension,
both in clarity and interest*

Allusion

Allusions make comparisons between similar things, suggesting more than the words actually say.

There is no odor so bad as that which arises from goodness tainted.

Analogy

Analogy is an extended metaphor or simile, making a comparison at length between two slighly different things.

The life in us is like the water in the river. It may rise this year higher than man has ever known it, and flood the parched uplands.

Atmosphere

Atmosphere is the feeling or mood in a piece of writing.

This delicious evening, when the whole body is one sense, and imbibes delight through every pore. I go and come with a strange liberty in Nature, a part of herself.

Conflict

Conflict is a struggle that the writing describes and attempts to resolve.

I weathered some merry snow-storms, and spent some cheerful winter evening by my fireside, while the snow whirled wildly without, and even the hooting of the owl was hushed.

Foreshadowing

Foreshadowing is the inclusion of hints and clues about the future.

Let us rise early and fast, gently and without perturbation; letcompany come and let company go, let the bells ring and the children cry - determined to make a day of it.

Hyperbole

Hyperbole is an exaggerated statement that the writer does not really expect to be believed.

The change from storm and winter to serene and mild weather, from dark and sluggish hours to bright and elastic ones, is a memorable crisis which all things proclaim.

Imagery

Imagery is descriptive language used to create a lively image of a person, situation, or setting.

He interested me because he was so quiet and solitary and so happy, a well of good humor and contentment which overflowed at his eyes.

Irony

Irony hides the intended meaning in words that signify the opposite of what is stated.

In October I went grape picking to the river meadows, and loaded myself with clusters more precious for their beauty and fragrance than for food.

Metaphor

Metaphors link unrelated images and ideas directly.

I looked out the window, and where yesterday was cold gray ice there lay the transparent pond already calm and full of hope as in a summer evening, reflecting a summer evening sky in its bosom, though none was visible overhead.

Personification

Personification gives human attributes to inanimate objects or concepts.

The sun, dispersing the mist, smiles on a checkered landscape of russet and white smoking with incense.

Realism

Realism is life depicted as it is in actuality.

At length the sun's rays have attained the right angle, and warm winds blow up mist and rain and melt the snowbanks.

Sensory Details

Sensory details create images related to the senses to describe a story or image.

Like the water, the Walden ice, seen near at hand, has a green tint, but at a distance is beautifully blue, and you can easily tell it from the white ice of the river, or the merely greenish ice of some ponds, a quarter of a mile off.

Simile

Similes link objects and ideas using "like" and "as".

The clouds cast shadows like giant trees on the mountains.

Tone

Tone shows the writer's feelings about the subject and may be happy, sad, calm, angry, funny or serious.

After reading and writing, in the forenoon, I usually bathed again in the pond, swimming across one of its coves, and washed the dust of labor from my person, or smoothed out the last wrinkle which study had made, and for the afternoon was absolutely free.

Understatement

Understatement deliberately states less than is intended, stating the opposite.

I went to the woods because I wished to live deliberately, to front only the essential facts of life, and see if I could not learn what it had to teach, and not, when I came to die, discover that I had not lived.
I had this advantage in my mode of life, over those who were obliged to look abroad for amusement, to society and the theater, that my life itself was become my amusement and never ceased to be novel. It was a drama of many scenes and without an end. If we were always getting our living, and regulating our lives according to the last and best mode we had learned, we should never be troubled with ennui.

In Wildness is the preservation of the World. Every tree sends its fibers forth in search of the Wild. I believe in the forest, and in the meadow, and in the night in which the corn grows. Give me the ocean, the desert, or the wilderness!

We had a remarkable sunset one day last November. I was walking in a meadow, the source of a small brook, when the sun at last, just before setting, after a cold, gray day, reached a clear stratum in the horizon, and the softest, brightest morning sunlight fell on the dry grass and on the stems of the trees in the opposite horizon and on the leaves of the shrub oaks on the hillside, while our shadows stretched long over the meadow eastward, as if we were the only motes in its beams. It was such a light as we could not have imagined a moment before, and the air also was so warm and serene that nothing was wanting to make a paradise of that meadow.

When we reflected that this was not a solitary phenomenon, never to happen again, but that it would happen forever and ever, an infinite number of evenings, and cheer and reassure the latest child that walked there, it was more glorious still. We walked in so pure and bright a light, gilding the withered grass and leaves, so softly and serenely bright, I thought I had never bathed in such a golden flood, without a ripple or murmer to it.

So we saunter toward the Holy Land, till one day the sun shall shine more brightly than ever he has done, shall perchance shine into our minds and hearts, and light up our whole lives with a great awakening light, as warm and serene and golden as on a bankside in autumn.

For more information and practice,

visit our website to see our other

English language services

beaumondelang1.com

Made in the USA
Lexington, KY
15 May 2014